WILLIAM WILBERFORCE

FREEDOM FIGHTER

WILLIAM WILBERFORCE

FREEDOM FIGHTER

BETTY STEELE EVERETT

CLC PUBLICATIONS

Fort Washington, PA 19034

• Freedom Fighter •

Published by CLC ❖ Publications

U.S.A.
P.O. Box 1449, Fort Washington, PA 19034

GREAT BRITAIN
51 The Dean, Alresford, Hants. SO24 9BJ

AUSTRALIA
P.O. Box 2299, Strathpine, QLD 4500

NEW ZEALAND
10 MacArthur Street, Feilding

ISBN 978-0-87508-976-8

Acknowledgments

Many people besides the author helped to produce this book.

The original idea for this biography of William Wilberforce came from the Publications Manager at Christian Literature Crusade, Ken Brown.

My son David Everett, Associate Director of duPont-Ball Library, Stetson University, Deland, Florida, helped with the initial research.

Others who sent me photocopied material or suggested additional sources include: Jacqueline Brown, Rembert E. Stokes Learning Resource Center, Wilberforce University, Wilberforce, Ohio; Jean K. Mulhern, Director, Wilberforce University Library, Wilberforce, Ohio; and Corinne Yeo, Wickford, Essex, England.

My sincere thanks to all these people.

Contents

1

From Cradle to Commons

IT WAS a warm August day in the seaside town of Hull, England. But in the large red brick house of merchant Robert Wilberforce, there were more important things to think about than the weather.

His wife, Elizabeth, had just had a baby. And after two daughters, this baby was a son!

"We'll name him for my father," Robert told his wife proudly. "William Wilberforce. This year of 1759 is a good time to be born English. Our army and navy are winning victories everywhere. We are going to be a world power with colonies all around the world!"

"Your father was mayor in Hull twice," Elizabeth reminded him. "Our little William will have a lot to live up to."

For a while, though, no one was sure little William would live at all. He was small and frail, and had trouble digesting food. But William did live. When he was seven he was sent to the local school. He was still small, and would later get the nickname "Shrimp." He also had poor eyesight, just as his mother did.

William had a sharp mind and an easygoing temperament. He could stay calm when other boys would get angry. He also had a good singing voice and could give dramatic and funny readings or mimic other people. These talents made him popular with almost everyone.

One of the people William met first at the school was Isaac Milner, an assistant teacher or "usher."

"His brother runs the school," the other boys told William. From the first day, William admired Isaac. To him, the nine year difference in their ages made Isaac a man. And he was everything William wanted to be, but already knew he never could be. Where William was small (he never would be much more than five feet tall), Isaac was big. Where William was frail and weak, Isaac was strong. William also admired Milner's knowledge and intelligence, especially when he heard that Milner had designed and built a sundial when he was only 8 years old. Young Milner had a good sense of humor, but he was serious about one thing: his religion.

It did not take Isaac long to recognize William's talents. He saw that his young student had a wonderful voice, and he came up with a way to use it to help all the boys at the school. "We'll put you up on a table," Isaac told William. "That way everyone can see and hear you. Then you can read out loud for the whole school. It'll be a lesson in elocution for them."

William did not mind having to stand on a table to be seen and heard. He loved having an audience because he knew he was a good reader and speaker. He had no trouble making the others pay attention to him. Even though he was small, William was well liked by the other boys, and they decided that listening to him read was more fun than studying!

William's school days at Hull did not last long. When he was only nine, his father died. His mother decided the best thing for William would be for him to go to stay with an aunt and uncle at Wimbledon. The uncle, whose name was also William, was Wilberforce's appointed guardian. Sadly William said goodbye to his friends at Hull School, including his friend Isaac Milner, and went to Wimbledon.

It didn't take William long to see that living with his aunt and uncle was going to be a lot different from living at home. William's mother had come from a leading family in Oxfordshire, and she liked the life of society. On the other hand, William's aunt was a follower of George Whitefield, one of the Methodists who were spreading out over the country. The things William's mother liked to do—playing cards, dancing, and going to the theater—were the very things his aunt and her friends thought were sinful!

William started in a new school, this one at Putney. He never thought he learned much there, but he liked living with his aunt and uncle. He began to think of them as his parents and did not mind the strictness of their religion. But again William was not to stay long in one place. About three years after he had come to Wimbledon, his mother came from London to take him home. She had heard about the strict religious views of William's aunt and decided this was no longer the place for her son! Although William felt sad to leave his aunt and uncle, he loved his mother, too.

"We will charm that serious spirit in you," William's mother promised. All of her friends seemed ready and willing to help her. At first William was upset by his friends' behavior and did not want to go with them to the theater, dances, card parties and huge suppers. Everyone paid attention to him, though, and William soon began to enjoy the fun and to forget that his aunt had taught him these things were wrong.

Naturally William had to go to school. This time

he went to the Grammar School of Pocklington. Here, for the first time, he heard about slavery. William had never seen a slave ship, nor been at an African depot where the blacks were brought to be loaded on the ships and taken to be sold, but he had a good imagination. Using his imagination, he wrote a letter to the editor of the *Yorkshire Gazette* condemning slavery.

By now William was a rich young man. His father, an uncle, and his grandfather had all died, leaving him money. His mother managed it for him.

The "Master" at Pocklington saw a good future for a young man with William's charm and ease and suggested he go on to St. John's College at Cambridge University. At the age of 17, William followed the suggestion and went to the University.

On his very first night there, William met a group of students who were looking for fun, not an education. They liked to drink and gamble, and they quickly decided that William should be one of them.

For his first year, William did stay with this group, but he was never really one of them. He may have been a little afraid of these older men, and he really did not approve of their lifestyle. Even though he was lively and outgoing, William also had a serious side.

Once rid of these men and their influence, William found plenty of other students eager to be friends with a young, attractive, amusing man with money to spend. Unfortunately, some of these new friends were William's tutors—the ones who were supposed to be teaching him and encouraging him to study, not play!

"Why would anyone with your money and brains bother studying?" they asked, trying to flatter him. "You do everything by real talent, not studying like the others have to!"

William was good in the classics and knew them in Greek and Latin. He also liked Shakespeare and his favorite poet was Cowper. In these subjects he did well on the exams without studying. But he was not very good in mathematics.

William liked being with people and did not like staying in his room. His mother approved of his partying lifestyle and was willing to give him his own money to spend on it. So William kept on with his life of amusement.

William Wilberforce's room became the gathering place for many students. He always kept a Yorkshire pie there, so anyone dropping in could have some. In his room, conversation, cards and games went on well into the morning on most nights.

The man who had rented the room next to William's was much more of a student. But even he fell under William's friendly spell. He would sometimes come to William's room, too, and always declared it was great fun to be there.

For three years William led this life of ease that his money allowed. He liked the fine clothes and other beautiful and comfortable things his money could buy. He even took to gambling for a time.

William, however, was too intelligent to believe all the flattery the tutors and others gave him. He did not study much at Cambridge, but he never thought he had nothing more to learn. When it was time to leave St. John's and Cambridge, William was asked, "What will you do now?"

There were a lot of ways a rich, popular young man could live and enjoy life, but William's serious side was finally beginning to come out. "I have three choices," William told himself. "I can have a life of pleasure. I can go into business. I can have a life of public service."

Already the life of nothing but fun and amusement was getting stale for William. Although he thought he would never give up the things he enjoyed, he also knew he did not want to make them his whole life anymore.

The merchant and banking house at Hull that had been his father's was giving William his income. But it was being well managed by his cousin, who wanted to keep doing his job there.

That left only a life of politics, or "public service," in William's mind. "I'll go back to Hull and stand [run] for the House of Commons," he decided. William was a born politician and knew how to get the people to vote for him. His opponents were two older men, both more experienced than he was, but that did not make William hesitate.

For his 21st birthday in August, 1780, William threw a big party at his home. The servants roasted a whole ox, and everyone in the area was invited to help celebrate William's coming of age. With so many people in one place, it was easy for William to talk to a lot of people and shake many hands.

"You knew my father and grandfather," he reminded the men as he mingled among them. Then he talked of the future for Hull, as well as the past. But William did not have to rely on his background or ancestors to influence the people. The charming young man was popular for himself. He was also able and willing to spend the money necessary to carry on a good campaign.

His best move, though, came between this party and the fall election. He went down to London where more than 300 "freemen" from Hull lived along the Thames River. William held big dinners at various public houses (inns or taverns) in the area and invited these men. There was plenty of food, beer and candlelight. While the men were eating and drinking, William would speak to them. He told them how much he loved his hometown, and he did it in a voice that always won people. Years later he would be called "The Nightingale of the House of Commons" because of his melodious voice.

William did not stop with merely winning votes for the election. He knew that he would have to know how things were done in the House of Commons if he was going to be a Member. So he began spending long nights in the galleries at Westminster. The galleries were balconies on each side of the House, held up by pillars. Spectators were allowed to sit there and listen to the debates on the House floor. Many of these debates were about the American War (the U.S. Revolution). Both sides were often bitter in their arguments and the debates became heated.

While William listened closely to the words of the speeches and studied how the debates were carried on, he became aware of another young man, about his own age, who was also sitting in the gallery, listening. This man was William Pitt, who, along with his father, was against the American War.

"We were at Cambridge together for a while," Pitt told William when they had introduced themselves. "But you were in St. John's College and I was in Pembroke." Pitt was too polite to add that he had spent his time at Cambridge studying, not partying. The friendship between the two men began then, and despite disagreements later in their lives, it lasted until Pitt's death.

When the election came in the fall, William Wilberforce received exactly the same number of votes as his two opponents together! William was off to London and the House of Commons. The stage was set for the next 45 years of his life.

2

Politics and Friendships

THE City of London and William Wilberforce were made for each other. The intrigue of politics in the Capital fascinated him, but he was especially fond of the give-and-take of the speeches and debates on the floor of the House of Commons.

It was all like a big game to William, and it was a game he loved because he was so good at it.

His gift of imitating people had always been appreciated by his friends at school, so William tried it in London. He imitated some of the political leaders, but this time his act was not appreciated. "Such actions do not help a young man just getting started in government," he was told firmly.

William took the advice. From then on he relied on his great speaking ability and ease with words to

win his points. He had so much talent in these that
it made it hard for the opposition to either snub
him or make fun of him. He quickly learned that if
he stayed inside the accepted limits of Parliamen-
tary behavior, he could say almost anything he
wanted about almost anyone in the government—
and get away with it! He did not need to mock anyone to win his points.

London, however, was more than just the Capital and center of government. It was also Britain's
center of the social life William liked so much. He
was soon involved in the lifestyle he had known at
home. He was invited to important events and was
welcome in the homes of the important people in
the City. He kept diaries that show how busy he
was and how popular he was with the social leaders.

Almost every night there was a many-course din-
ner at someone's big house. Expensively dressed la-
dies and gentlemen ate delicacies such as duck, turtle,
venison and asparagus, served at beautifully set
tables.

There were also dances, card parties and the opera, all usually followed by a late supper. Often William did not get to bed before two or three in the
morning after one of these nights out.

But he was paying a physical price for this fast-
paced, glamorous life. William's diaries show days
when he wrote "feverish" and other days when he

put down "very much fatigued." None of this was enough to make the young man change his lifestyle and schedule, though, and he began to have trouble sleeping at night. One time, after spending the night in a friend's home, William wrote that he had been kept awake by fleas! More often, though, it was his own thinking and planning for the debates coming up in the House that kept William awake at night.

William's eyesight was slowly getting worse. Sometimes, after a long night of playing cards, or because of cold or dusty weather, it would be so bad that he had trouble seeing to write in his diary, and the lines ran together.

One of the best things about this time in William's life was his friendship with William Pitt. His friend had also been elected to the House, from another district. The two newcomers had a lot in common. They had many of the same friends and so were invited to many of the same events. They both enjoyed the sharp and witty conversation that was a big part of a gentleman's life in the days before radio, television and movies.

There were also serious differences between the two Williams. Pitt was taller and walked as straight as a soldier on parade. Wilberforce was already getting the rounded shoulders and bent walk that come from being near-sighted.

Their personalities were as different as their physical characteristics. Pitt was a serious and determined young man; Wilberforce was more impulsive and emotional and could be either highly elated or deeply depressed. He had a charm some people thought was almost like a woman's in its grace and sensibility. These traits let him laugh and cry more easily than the steady Pitt could.

With their differences, the two men balanced and helped each other. Pitt showed Wilberforce the serious side of politics, a side in which the good of the people and the country came before just "winning" at the game of debate. At the same time, he helped William come to think the same way he did about the issues being debated in the House of Commons.

On the other side, William helped Pitt learn to relax and unwind a little. He introduced him to some of the social life and clubs in which he was so active. While Pitt never could show his emotions in public the way Wilberforce could, he did learn from his friend to join in the fun when he was with close friends.

Once the two Williams began serving in the House of Commons, it was quickly obvious to everyone that Pitt would be the future star of government. Wilberforce, who now held almost the same political views, would be his loyal supporter.

Pitt's first speech in the House was outstanding. William knew he could not hope to equal it, even with all his wit and charm. His own "maiden speech" (or first speech) came in the House on May 17, 1781. William attacked the current revenue laws. In his second speech he criticized the government for not making the Navy bigger. He reminded his listeners that Hull had a great capacity for building ships. William had not forgotten who had elected him to Parliament or what district he represented!

Both Pitt and Wilberforce were against the "American War," now being fought across the Atlantic to a losing end for England. When William Wilberforce spoke in the House on a motion to end the war, he told the Ministers bluntly that they had managed the whole war in a "cruel, bloody, and impractical manner."

Although William saw that Pitt had more ability to lead than he did, he was not jealous. Right after Pitt's first speech, William wrote to a friend that he expected someday to see Pitt the Prime Minister of England. It was a prediction that came true a few years later.

About this time, William got word that his uncle in Wimbledon had died. This was the man who had helped raise William when he was a child, and he left his nephew even more money and the house in Wimbledon.

The house was big, with enough room for eight or ten guests to stay overnight. It was also close

enough to London to let William live there and com-
mute to Parliament.

"You'll be able to have lots of friends visit you,"
William was told. He did entertain lavishly in his
new home, and one of the most familiar faces there
was Pitt's, as he enjoyed William's food, drink and
company.

In December of 1783, William Pitt did become
Prime Minister, at the age of only 24. Many people
expected Pitt to offer his friend Wilberforce a special post in his government, but Pitt never did. No
one was quite sure why William had been passed
over, but William apparently understood Pitt's position. Pitt was not popular with the House of Commons, and he counted heavily on William's support there. William was more valuable to Pitt in the
House than in the inner circle of government.

Several times later in his life, William would seem
to be close to being made a Minister in the government. Once it was so certain in people's minds that
the companies who designed and made the robes
for the officials wanted to begin work on some for
William!

Not being in Pitt's government was all right with
William. Being out of the government circle meant
he was free to think and vote as he wanted to in
Parliament. If William had been a Minister, he
would have had to go along with the ideas and opin-

ions of the leaders even if he did not agree with them.

During his short time in the House, Pitt had made enemies. There were many who wanted to see him thrown out of office and out of the Prime Minister's home at Number 10 Downing Street.

In the House, William led the fight for his friend. The "game" of trying to hold off Pitt's enemies was exciting, but the battle in the House was a losing one. In March of 1784, Pitt had to give in and call for an election. (In England elections are held whenever the King or Queen, at the Prime Minister's request, dissolves Parliament. The people then vote to either support or reject the Prime Minister and his party.)

William was in Yorkshire, the largest county in England, at that time. He was speaking at an all-day political meeting. He was running in the election there against strong opposition.

The weather did not cooperate. It was a cold day, with rain, wind and even hail. William was to speak near the end of the day, and by the time he crawled up onto the table for his speech the men in the crowd were cold and tired and ready to call it a day.

The speakers were partly protected by a wooden canopy, but even so, William's small frame was hit hard by the wind. William did not let that bother him. He spoke for an hour, and his audience hung on every word. One of these listeners was James

Boswell, who later told a friend, "I saw what seemed a mere shrimp mount upon the table, but as I listened, he grew and grew, until the shrimp became a whale."

Boswell's description of William was a good one. People forgot his size when he started to speak. In the next years, Boswell's words were repeated many times.

William was well into his speech when he was interrupted by a messenger from London carrying a note from Pitt. William scanned the note quickly, letting the tension build as the crowd whispered about what might be in the message. Then William waved it dramatically over his head. "Pitt appeals to you!" he shouted, and read them the news that Parliament had been dissolved and there would be an election.

The only part of the note William did not read was the private ending from his friend. Pitt had written only to William, "Take care to keep all our friends together and to tear the enemy apart!"

The crowd cheered the news of the coming election. Somewhere, someone started a chant. "Wilberforce! Wilberforce! Wilberforce for us!" Others picked up the cry, and in a few minutes everyone was screaming William's name at the top of their lungs. They wanted William to represent Yorkshire, not Hull, in the House of Commons from now on.

The people of York had been so impressed with William's speeches, personality and style that they elected him their representative in a landslide victory. Pitt too was a winner, ready to head the government again.

When Parliament reopened, William was no longer a "little" member from Hull. He was now one of the most important members because he represented the largest county in the nation. And he was also a close friend of the Prime Minister who was now solidly established in his position.

But the coming year was to see an even bigger change in William's life. It was a change that was not political, but it would influence his work in Parliament from then on.

3

Face to Face with Jesus

IT WAS William's 25th birthday, and he had big plans for the day. "First the races at York," he decided, "and then I'll go down to Scarborough."

At Scarborough, William suddenly spotted a familiar face in the crowd. He had not seen the man for years, but he recognized him immediately. "Isaac Milner!" he shouted, and waved to his old teacher from Hull.

William knew that Milner was now a Don (or Professor) at Cambridge, as well as a Christian minister. But Milner was even bigger than William remembered. His size dwarfed the younger man as they stood talking.

"I have an idea," William said suddenly. "We're leaving for a trip to France. My mother, my sister and two female cousins are going. But I'm the only male. Why don't you join us? We men could ride in one carriage, the women in another. It would be a good time to talk."

Milner quickly agreed. He liked France, and he liked the idea of renewing his friendship with William now that he was a man too.

It did not take many miles before the men realized they had made a good choice in traveling together. Not only were they different in appearance, but William was casual and interested in having fun whenever and wherever possible. Isaac was far more serious and religious.

Whenever Milner would bring up religion or his beliefs, though, William would laugh and ridicule them. Milner finally admitted that he was no match for William, but that if he really wanted to talk seriously about the subject, he would be glad to talk with him.

After a short time with the women in southern France, the two men left them at a house for the winter and started back to England together. Travel in a horse-drawn carriage was slow in the best of weather, but now snow and bad roads slowed the men even more. Because the inns along the way were usually dirty and served poor quality food, the carriage would leave before dawn and travel until dark.

Along the way, the carriage came to a steep hill

covered with ice. The driver stopped and looked over the situation. "You'll have to get out and walk," he said. "We have to ease the load on the horses."

William and Isaac got out and began to climb slowly behind the carriage. The horses were having trouble walking on the slippery ice. Suddenly the driver shouted a warning. "Look out! The carriage is sliding back!" Milner grabbed the carriage, dug in his heels and with all the strength in his big body held on. The slide stopped, and on their next try the horses made it to the top of the hill.

The men got back into the carriage, but William kept thinking about what had happened. He and Isaac had come close to being killed!

During the long hours in the carriage there was nothing for the men to do but talk or read. Both liked to read and both were good talkers. They discussed a lot of different things, but they always seemed to come back to religion. William discovered that his old teacher was now an "Evangelical," believing the same things that the Methodists believe. These believers were interested in personal religion and living like Jesus. They did not believe that merely going to church was enough to be a true Christian.

"I have a book I think is one of the best ever written," Isaac told his friend. He held up a copy of *The Rise and Progress of Religion in the Soul.* It was not a new book. It had been published forty years before by Philip Doddridge, a Nonconformist minister. William was impressed with Isaac's praise of the book, and the two men began to read it together. They then discussed what they had read as their carriage bounced along the rough roads.

More and more, William was coming to admire Isaac himself. The book, and the things his old teacher said, made him start to think seriously about his own Christianity and to wonder where he really stood with God.

For the next year, though, William made no great changes in his life. He continued to think about religion, but he kept on with his frivolous lifestyle.

A year later, William asked Isaac to go back to France with him to bring the women home. This time the two men read the New Testament in Greek as they rode, discussing what was written. "What are you two doing up there?" William's mother complained once. "You don't come back to visit our carriage enough!"

William did not want his mother to know that he was slowly coming to believe the way Isaac did. He had not forgotten how she had pulled him away from his aunt and uncle in Wimbledon when he was a boy, and he was afraid she would try to get him away from his serious thinking about religion now too.

"You must talk to John Newton," Isaac told William several times when questions came up. "He was master of a slave ship when he was converted. Now he is Rector of St. Mary Woolnoth on Lombard Street."

William frowned. "I think my aunt knew him. You say he was master of a slave ship?"

"Yes, and he's a friend of your favorite poet, Cowper. In fact, Newton has written two beautiful hymns himself: 'How Sweet the Name of Jesus Sounds' and 'Glorious Things of Thee are Spoken.' I'm sure he'll be writing more. But I warn you, he does not look like a poet! He's a homely man!"

William was not sure he wanted to talk to this converted slaver who was the leader of the "Evangelicals." What if Newton convinced him to believe what he did and to become more than just a churchgoing Christian? "I might have to give up all the fun and good things," William thought. "And what would my friends say if I became 'evangelical' and 'religious'? They might not like me or want me around anymore!"

William also wondered what would happen to his political career if he joined Newton's group. Would the people reelect him to the House of Commons, or would they turn against him if he became religious?

William was depressed and deeply aware of his

own guilt before God. But he loved being in the House of Commons and knew he was popular there. What if he was voted out because he became "religious"? He was not sure he wanted to pay so high a price for following Milner and Newton.

At last William decided to go to Lombard Street to hear John Newton preach. He arranged to meet the former slaver privately. "Don't tell anyone I'm coming," William wrote Newton. "I'll come after dark. Someone might recognize me if I came in the daylight."

When the men met, Newton spoke bluntly. "I'm the 'Old African Blasphemer.'"

Now sixty years old, Newton's life had been almost completely opposite from William's life of wealth and ease. "I was impressed into the Navy when I was just a boy," Newton said. "I tried to desert and was flogged, so I know all about hard discipline. I got into the slave trade when I got the job of overseer at a Gold Coast depot in Africa. That's where they bring the blacks to be shipped out as slaves."

"How did you get to be master of a slave ship?" William asked.

"A friend of my father's finally brought me back to England. I worked as a mate on a slaver, but I finally got a ship of my own."

Newton kept William both shocked and spellbound with his stories of cruelty to the blacks. He told in detail how the Africans were branded, then jammed into the slave ships so tightly that they could barely move except when brought up on deck for exercise. He told about the beatings and other inhumane punishments, and of the deaths—and how the bodies were dumped into the ocean without any religious service or attention. He showed William drawings he had made that showed how the Africans were treated.

"Being in the slave trade was a pit!" Newton declared. "And my Creator lifted me from it! I will serve Him all my days!"

Newton admitted that even after he was converted, he had not stopped his work in the slave trade. In those days slavery was accepted because people made so much money from it. But Newton changed things so that his ships were kept clean and the slaves were treated humanely.

Shortly after his conversion, however, Newton began feeling that God had better use for his talents. His health was not as good as it once was, and he decided to give up slaving completely.

Newton also told William about the religious group he now led. "There are less than a hundred of us now. We're called "Evangelicals" or the "Evangelical Party," but we're not a political party. We're just a group of men in government and the Church who share the same Christian beliefs. We want to reform the manners and morals of the English people. Our aim is to bring the people true religion."

Soon after his talk with Newton, William became a Christian and began to develop a relationship with the Lord. As a result he began spending several hours a day, usually in the early morning, studying the Bible. He stopped doing some of the things on Sunday that he had been enjoying, and he dropped his membership in some clubs. He also cleaned up his vocabulary.

"What will my friends think?" William wondered again. Some of his old friends did turn away, but new friends, who thought as he did now, came to take their places. Most of William's old friends, although bored by anyone who was enthusiastic about religion, still accepted him because he was charming and witty. And he did not force his new views too hard on them.

"Should I resign from the House of Commons?" William asked Newton. It was the question most on his mind. Newton shook his head. "Stay where you are and try to make changes through the law and government. We need men like you in Commons."

William was still afraid he would lose his seat, but he soon understood that God had led him at the right time to become a Christian. Before his first election people would not have voted for him if he had been religious. Now they knew and admired him, so they were ready to vote for him again.

William also admitted in his diary that he could not continue some of the campaign tactics he had used before his conversion.

With the conversion of William Wilberforce, God had provided the Evangelicals with the most important thing they needed and did not have: a true leader in government.

The Wesleys, who had started "Methodism," appealed to the lower and middle classes. But William was not only an important member of Parliament, he was also rich and knew all the country's leaders personally. Through William Wilberforce, God gave Newton and his friends an opening into the inner circle of government and society that none of them had been able to make for themselves. Now it was time to use the advantages the Evangelical Party had.

4

The War Against Slavery Begins

THIS TIME when William went back to the House of Commons he was a different man. He was welcomed back by the other men who thought of themselves as the "Evangelical Party."

It was not really a political party. The men belonged to different political parties, but they were all Christians like William. Although there were not many of them, they always voted the same way on moral issues, choosing what they thought God would want for the country. "Our only question on any bill is, 'Is it morally right?'" they told William. "The others call us 'The Saints' because of how we try to live and vote."

Later, as William became the leader of this group, he would be called the "leader of the Saints."

But things were happening that William did not know about. These were things that would start him on his long fight to free the slaves.

Sir Charles Middleton, Controller of the Navy, and his wife felt strongly about the evils of slavery. They agreed, though, that any action would have to come through Parliament to have any lasting effect. "We'll go down through the names of Members to find someone to help us," the Middletons decided.

At the name of William Wilberforce they stopped. "This is our man!"

In 1787 William got a letter from the Middletons, asking him to bring up the matter of slavery in the House of Commons. William did not hesitate. "I feel unequal to the task," he wrote back, "but I could not possibly decline, because I feel the great importance of the subject."

Actually, slavery in England itself had been outlawed 14 years before when 14,000 slaves were freed, thanks to the work of the anti-slavery movement. But this law only freed the slaves living in England. The slave trade to the colonies kept right on, and the trade in blacks with other countries meant slavery was still being practiced almost all around the world.

By the summer of 1787, the "Committee for the Abolition of the Slave Trade" had been formed. They too were looking for someone in Parliament to speak for them. Again, William Wilberforce was the choice.

But the final nudge to William came from William Pitt. In the spring, Pitt, his cousin Grenville and William were at Pitt's home. It was a warm day, so they went outside to lounge under a big oak tree. Pitt looked at William. Calling him by the nickname only a very few close friends used, he said, "Wilber, why don't you give notice of a motion on the subject of the slave trade?"

With so much urging, William Wilberforce's goal was set from then on. Later, when asked how he got into the fight against slavery, he always remembered that day and Pitt's question as the start.

The problem was how to bring up the subject in the House. Slavery was an important part of the trade system in England. The country had lost its American colonies by war. Now more than ever it needed the colonies it still had in the West Indies. The planters in these colonies sent money to England. They traded with England. They bought and sold votes with their money. And all of this depended on the work of slaves and the slave trade.

A major British trading route was from England to Africa, then the Americas and back to England. Ships reached Africa laden with copper and iron bars, cloth, firearms, liquor and cheap trinkets. These were bartered for black people who had been captured, put in chains and brought to the coast. Many of them were taken to the West Indies and were there sold to the planters. Then the ships returned to England carrying sugar, an expensive luxury item which the British people loved. This was no small business.

William knew that if he brought up anti-slave bills, it could mean the end of his career in the House of Commons. But he was not being led by what would be good for William Wilberforce. Now he was being led by a much higher Power.

William and his friends decided to talk to the Quakers. They had had an Abolition Committee for a long time.

"How should we go about this?" William and the others asked the Quakers.

"There must be three themes," they were told. "The first is the wrongs done to the African continent. The second is the horrors of the slave trade. The last is the evils of slavery itself."

The movement against slavery appealed to all Christians regardless of their denomination. It united them against a common enemy, and most Christian groups were already trying to reach out to the slaves to help them find Christ.

Even with his intense work in the slavery battle, William was not forgetting his other main interest: moral improvement in England. In the fall of that year he put his thoughts down in his journal: "God has set before me two great objectives: the suppression of the slave trade and the reformation of manners." "Manners" meant "morals," which were at a low point in England. The fight to change and make them better would be another lifelong battle for William.

While William's ultimate goal was to end slavery in the British Empire completely, he knew that sudden and immediate emancipation was not practical. It would not be approved by the House, it would throw the economy of many parts of the country into chaos, and it would free slaves who were not able to take care of themselves. A different plan was needed.

William reasoned that if no ships were allowed to carry the slaves from Africa, there would be no new slaves to buy and sell. If the supply of slaves was cut off, the whole practice would ultimately end. This would happen gradually, which would help the planters get used to not having slaves to work their plantations.

William gave notice that he would introduce a motion in the House in the new session, a bill to abolish the slave trade. While his friends were eager, and others seemed willing to back his resolution, John Wesley (now 84 years old) wrote to warn William that the opposition would use both money and arguments to fight him.

William's poor health was also his enemy. He got sick, and even though he tried to keep working on the campaign from bed, he could not. Exhaustion, fever and loss of sleep and appetite made him even sicker. The doctors were worried and shook their heads. "He won't last twelve months."

"He won't last two weeks," others said. "Send for his relatives!"

But William was a fighter in his body as well as his mind, and he was determined to live. In a month he had come through the crisis. The doctors then ordered him to go to Bath, a popular hot springs resort where he would "take the waters." Everyone believed that the waters at Bath could heal people. William would both bathe in and drink them. The treatments here had helped William before, so he went again.

But leaving London right now meant that William would have to ask someone else to take over his work on the Slave Trade Bill in the House. William Pitt was the one who moved that the House investigate the slave trade, although coming out in favor of the bill was a dangerous political move for him.

John Wesley's warning about the opposition's fight was not an idle one. At the beginning, one man showed William a picture of the crucifixion, saying that this was what happened to young reformers.

Some members of the House did not want to make any changes. They wanted everything to stay the way it was. They were fearful that the changes William wanted would affect their comfortable lives.

Most people in England at this time did not realize what terrible cruelty the slaves experienced, because the people had not seen the slaves' conditions firsthand. Besides, life for the British common people was also cruel in many ways. Courts imposed harsh punishments, such as public floggings, for very minor crimes. Other white prisoners were sent to penal colonies in Australia. As a result, many people felt that the slaves' conditions could not be much worse than their own, and they had little interest in helping the slaves.

Some of the people against William's bill were national heroes. Even Lord Nelson, who was popular because of his defeat of Napoleon at the Battle of Trafalgar, was against stopping the slave trade.

In addition, the slave trade was profitable. An investor could often make a 100 percent gain on his money. Not only the wealthy, but also many in the working class were making a great deal of money in this way.

Those opposing Williams' reforms knew that the most important thing for them to do was keep the question of humanity and fair treatment out of the debate. Recently, a court decision had come after an incident at sea when a captain had thrown shackled slaves overboard to lighten the load. The law had ruled that slaves were only property and that the captain could do with them whatever he wanted, as he could with his cows and horses.

Merchants dealing in slaves painted a falsely favorable picture of slave conditions. "The slave ships are happy places," they told House Members. "The blacks sing because they are thankful for the chance to leave barbarous Africa to come to Christian countries."

Unfortunately for these merchants, a slave ship was being fitted out right then on the River Thames.

"We'll go down and see for ourselves," some of the Members said.

They came back with tales of gross cruelty to the black slaves. The other Members, including Pitt, were so shocked that they readily passed a bill to ease the treatment of slaves on the ships. And the next month, after much opposition, the bill was also approved by the House of Lords. But both Houses of Parliament voted against abolishing the slave trade altogether.

For the next few months, England had other national problems. The slave trade bills were mostly forgotten. But the next year William brought up the subject again.

William was still not feeling well when he got to London, but he spoke to the House for three and a half hours—all without notes! He tried hard to concentrate on attacking slavery itself rather than attacking those who supported it.

One of the other men who spoke for abolition was James Stephen. This young lawyer, who would later marry one of William's sisters, had seen two Negroes burned to death in the West Indies. The House listened and then talked about the subject for nine days. They ended by setting up a committee to hear arguments during the summer—and then adjourned.

William knew that he and his friends had a lot of work to do before the next session if they were to end the slave trade. His home became the meeting place for the Slave Committee.

"They are Wilber's 'white Negroes,'" Pitt commented about the committee. But they were men of intelligence and influence, and they were all solidly behind William in his fight.

The Abolitionists were gaining support from the people now. One man made a model of a slave ship showing how 450 blacks were packed in like fish in a can. William Cowper, the great poet, wrote "The Negro's Complaint," and Josiah Wedgwood, the famous potter, made a cameo of a Negro in chains engraved with the words "Am I Not a Man and a Brother?"

The Abolition Society flooded the country with pamphlets, trying to educate the people about the slave trade. William was one of the first to see the power of these pamphlets to influence and educate the people as well as the Members of the Houses of Parliament.

But William and his friends had a major setback. Slaves in Santo Domingo revolted against their white masters. Perhaps these slaves had heard of the anti-slavery movement in England. Perhaps they hoped to take advantage of that movement by furthering their own cause. At any event, the stories that came back to England were graphic pictures of blood-crazed slaves burning, looting and committing savage acts.

The revolt in Santo Domingo also frightened the planters in Jamaica. There the blacks outnumbered the white population 16 to 1, and the planters and owners blamed William for the situation in Santo Domingo. The planters were definitely not on William's side!

In April of 1791 William spoke to the House again. In a four-hour speech he told of the horrors of the slave trade. He had learned a lot more about the harsh treatment of the Africans, both while they were on the ships and after they had been sold.

"They prefer death to slavery!" he shouted. "They will jump overboard from the ships; and when they are in the agonies of death, they will hold up their hands in joy for having escaped their tormentors!"

He also described in his elegant voice the whippings, and even the holding of red-hot coals to the lips of slaves who were trying to starve themselves to death. One of William's most horrible examples was that of a six-year-old girl whose master had cut her mouth from ear to ear.

William understood, though, that telling about the horrors and torture of the blacks was not enough. The Members of the House had to see how the slave trade was affecting whites too. He quoted from the muster rolls of seamen from Liverpool and Bristol to make his point: "In one year, out of 12,263 seamen in the slave trade, 2,643 have died!"

Despite William's passionate speech, his description of the cruelty to slaves and his figures on dying seamen, the motion was defeated by a vote of 88 to 163. William responded by vowing to bring up the issue every year until the slave trade was abolished.

William kept his promise. The next twenty years would be constant hard work to abolish slavery. That work would make William Wilberforce one of the most loved men in England—and one of the most hated!

5

The Evangelicals

WILLIAM Wilberforce did continue his fight against the slave trade. A lot of men, if they talked so much about one thing, might have been ignored or disliked by the others in the House of Commons. But William had a personality and talents that kept him popular.

First of all, he was funny. In the House, where the speeches were almost always long and very dull, the Members knew that when it was William who was to speak, they would be able to laugh and enjoy the time. It was a change they looked forward to, even when they disagreed completely with what he said.

Also, although William had a great talent for sarcasm, everyone knew he was too kindhearted to use it except in rare and unusual situations. He was more eager to compromise and to use diplomacy than he was to use threats and personal pressure on the opposition.

Anti-slave trade and abolition bills from William came to be expected by the other Members. When he tried again in 1792, the word "gradual" was put before "abolition." Knowing that the slaves would not be freed immediately but slowly, made the bill a lot easier for many Members to accept. It was passed by the House of Commons.

The "Saints" were elated.

"The trade's finally been officially condemned," they congratulated each other.

But their victory and joy did not last long. The bill was defeated in the House of Lords.

Soon after this, William's life was threatened twice by captains of West Indian slave ships. One hated William because he had humiliated him in cross-examination during the anti-slave debate. He challenged William to a duel. William discussed the situation with his friends, but he apparently never seriously considered dueling. It was a practice he detested, and he felt it was not Christian to try to kill another man.

The other threat to William's life came from a Captain Kimber. During the debate for the bill, William had named some of the officers who had been responsible for the most recent and worst atrocities against the slaves on their ships. Captain Kimber had whipped a pregnant fifteen-year-old girl to death for no apparent reason.

After the debate in the House, Kimber was tried for murder and was found not guilty. He was not satisfied, and he wrote to William demanding money, a public apology and a job in government. Naturally, William rejected all three demands. Kimber began coming to William's house and way-laying him on the street where he would shout insults and threats at him.

"You need armed bodyguards," said William's worried friends. "We can't protect you!"

As usual William took a different, softer view. "I really believe that if he were to commit any act of violence, it would be beneficial rather than injurious to our cause." Eventually, another Member of the House talked Kimber into leaving William alone, and the threat was over.

Physical attacks and threats were not the only means William's enemies used to upset him and try to stop his work for the slaves. He was always being criticized by someone somewhere. It didn't matter if the "facts" were right or not, and many of the stories that were started about him were fantastic.

Although William was not married, the rumor was started that his wife was black. When this was not enough, another report accused him of being a wife beater!

The most serious charge against William was that he was willing to fight for black slaves who lived hundreds of miles from him but ignored the conditions of the poor whites at home. These enemies called William a hypocrite who did not want to abolish slavery as much as he wanted to use the fight for his own personal advancement in politics. One newspaper wrote that William would do better to help the British laboring classes. The writer added, "They would be happy to lick the dishes and bowls out of which the black slaves have breakfasted, dined, or supped."

It was true that the poor in England lived under harsh conditions. They worked long hours at tedious and sometimes dangerous work for very little pay. But while William never worked openly to improve these conditions, he gave money to help establish schools for the poor and worked to do away with child labor.

Most of William's enemies did not understand that his interest in abolishing slavery was basically a religious one. No one person can fight all of the evils of the world at the same time; William had been called by God to fight slavery. God would raise up others to fight different injustices.

Many of William's attackers had more personal reasons for accusing him. He had never bothered to flatter important people, and he did what he believed to be right even if his views were unpopular.

William did not reply publicly to any of these charges. Any hurt he felt at them he kept to himself, "talking" only to his journal.

In 1793 William tried again to get a bill through the House of Commons that would keep British ships from carrying slaves to foreign countries. The bill was not passed. He tried again in 1795 without success. But in 1796 he was hopeful that this would be the time his bill would be passed by the House.

On the evening of the vote, when William got to the House of Commons, he found it almost empty. Especially missing were the Members he had been counting on to vote with him. He had no idea why they were not in their places—and his bill was defeated again.

Later, when William checked to find out why so many of his backers had been away for the vote, he found out that the opposition had given them free tickets to a very popular opera. They had been in the theater, not in the House, when it was time to vote on the bill!

During these years of fighting for abolition, William was also working to raise the morals of his country. While doing so he met Hannah More, a playwright who was also working for the Evangelical cause by writing pamphlets. William and Hannah became good friends, and their friendship lasted throughout their lives.

The "Saints" had decided, in 1792, to move closer together, and they chose the village of Clapham as their center. They hoped that this close community life would help all of them to strengthen their personal commitment to God. They also wanted to strengthen their political position, hoping that this would hasten the moral reforms they were seeking.

One of the leaders of the Evangelicals was Henry Thornton, and it was his home that was selected to be the center for the group. His home had been remodeled several times and now had 34 bedrooms. For several years, William was one of the men who lived there. It was an impressive building. The estate's library became the "command center" for the community. Smaller houses were built in the estate's gardens, and in a few years several of William's closest friends had homes there. Others, like Hannah More, visited often.

The "Clapham Sect," as others called the group, carried a lot of power in politics. They were more modern than most men of their day. They allowed their wives and children to have a full part in activities. The "Clapham Sect" was interracial and stressed complete equality. White and black children played together. The black youths were the children of chiefs in Sierra Leone, a colony in Africa which had been established by freed slaves with help from the Abolitionists. For a time, William was on its Board of Directors.

William was actively involved with many "societies," which were organizations that promoted particular causes. Some of these causes may seem strange to us today, such as one society which was founded to encourage people not to use bad language. Other societies promoted social reform, such as improving education for the poor and increasing the number of policemen patrolling the streets. William gave money to many of these societies, perhaps as many as 100 of them. He also served as president, vice president or committee member for at least 60 societies.

From the time he became a Christian until he retired from politics, William was a speaker at almost every meeting held for a moral cause. People came just to see and hear him. "Where does he find time to prepare so many speeches?" people wondered. William always found time for anything he believed in.

But the fight to raise morals was as hard as the battle to end slavery. The English upper class saw no reason to change their lives. Wasn't England the top power in the world? Didn't they have colonies around the globe? They argued that they were at the highest possible level of civilization. These people would not admit that their comforts and "civilization" were built on the slave trade, child labor, poverty and illiteracy for most people and corruption in high places. Even Church positions were bought and sold.

The upper class ignored the harsh treatment of criminals and the lack of law and order on the streets. They argued that employing more policemen would mean repression, not protection. But they had their servants to protect them.

Wilberforce was ridiculed in cartoons in the newspapers, and many people were suspicious of him. But he did not change his goals. He spent his own money when he felt it was needed—usually for schools for the poor, or for churches.

William's generosity was often spontaneous. When he saw someone in need, he could not keep from helping. Often he knew, even as he handed over his money, that it would probably be wasted or spent for something else, but he still had to give it!

Missions were always close to William's heart. One of the men he admired most was the energetic Baptist missionary William Carey. Carey had gone to India where he eventually translated the Bible into six languages and established a Christian college.

When Wilberforce learned that Bibles were hard to get, both in England and abroad, he joined with the Reverend Charles Thomas in founding The British and Foreign Bible Society. The government would not give money for this, and the churches were too poor to do it. So William contacted people of various churches and occupations to give money to buy Bibles to give to the people.

The thing that bothered William most was that missionaries were not encouraged to go to India, which was then a British colony. The English residents did not want those at home in England to realize they took advantage of the nationals. The Indians used as servants were not paid well and were harshly treated in the courts.

Next to the slave trade, Wilberforce believed, the fact that Christian teaching was banned in India was one of the "worst blots on our country's image." It took until 1813 to win the freedom to bring Christian missionaries and religion to India, but William and his friends finally won that fight.

Even though he was working hard for others, William knew how important it was to see to his own Christian growth and witness. He was always trying to think of ways to bring his beliefs into any conversation. He called this "honest bait" to get the attention of his acquaintances who thought they had everything. The friend William most wanted to see have the same experience that he had had after visiting John Newton, was William Pitt.

To remind himself to keep his mind on heavenly things, William sometimes slipped a pebble into his shoe. Every step brought pain and a reminder to concentrate on God.

For several years William used his diary to grade himself on such things as his prayers, self-denial, the company he kept, his conversations and a number of other things he thought he needed to do to be a better Christian. Each day he would give himself a grade on how he had done in each category the day before. He was not an easy grader! There were only a few "better" or "better, I hope" ratings. Most areas got "need to be improved" and other low grades.

Despite his strong convictions, William was still popular in upper class circles. He was not self-conscious about what he believed, and this helped make him feel more comfortable around people.

While William's work to free the slaves and uplift the morals of England took all his time, something was about to happen that would change his life completely. And, again, it was not political.

6

Love and Marriage

ALL HIS adult life William had been busy. He had his work in the House of Commons, his active social life and his many charitable works. He had many friends in the Clapham Sect and among the Evangelicals. He had concluded that he did not have time for anything new in his busy life. But suddenly he realized that something important and pleasant was missing.

William was now 38 years old. Most of his friends were married, with families. As he saw their happiness and joy in having a wife and children to come home to, William knew he wanted that too.

Although his good nature and charm had always made William attractive to women, he knew he was not good-looking. His eyesight was getting worse. He had to have a reader read most things to him now. He was short and round-shouldered. Although he had many women friends, he had never considered having a romantic relationship with any of them.

"I am thinking of marriage," William suddenly announced one day to his friend, Thomas Babington.

"And I know just the girl for you!" Thomas replied eagerly. He was excited that William was thinking about getting married. "Her name is Barbara Spooner! She's twenty years old and is the oldest daughter of a banker at Birmingham. She's very religious too."

Within a few days, William received a letter from Barbara. In the letter she mentioned a spiritual concern and asked for his advice. William felt that hearing from Barbara so soon after her name had been mentioned by his friend could not be a coincidence. He decided to meet Barbara.

On April 15, 1797, the two met. William fell immediately and deeply in love, and Barbara was attracted to him too. "This is the woman God wants me to marry," William said confidently. At the age of 38, William did not want to waste time on a long courtship as was considered "proper" at that time. By April 23 he had proposed to Barbara and she had accepted. They were married on May 30.

The Wilberforces did not have a long honeymoon. William did not want to spend time on frivolous things, so he took Barbara on a tour of the Sunday schools and day schools that Hannah More and her sisters had begun.

Actually, the idea for these schools had been William's own. He had been visiting Hannah a few years before and commented that while the scenery in the region was delightful, the spiritual situation of the people was not. Hannah needed no more encouragement than that. She and her sisters began the schools for the poor. With the money William gave them, they made these schools models for many others that came later in different parts of England.

Barbara Wilberforce was an attractive woman with dark hair and eyes. But she was not physically strong. Nor was she popular with the other women in William's large circle of friends. The other women thought she was a poor housekeeper and hostess, a complainer who whined when William was not right beside her, and that she was too tight with money.

William, however, saw nothing but good in his wife. He cheerfully admitted that she was too frail to worry about things around the house, and he entrusted all the housework to the servants. A kind-hearted woman, Barbara fussed over William, worrying about his health and his many speaking engagements. While he was always cheerful, Barbara was often depressed and pessimistic. She finally worried herself into very bad health which lasted the rest of her life.

But Barbara's worry about William's health probably helped him. She insisted that he stop eating meals out so often, get to bed earlier and walk more. It all helped to conserve his energy for his work.

The newlyweds bought an estate, Broomhill, near William's friends. They had 13 or 14 servants, which was average for people as wealthy and important as the Wilberforces. But there was something unique about the servants William hired. None of them had been hired because they knew how to do their jobs. They had all been hired because they were badly in need of work and could not get jobs anywhere else!

James Burningham was a typical servant of the Wilberforces. After he had been William's secretary for five years he became sick. His eyes began to fail too. William had him treated and kept him at home for fifteen months. But, although his illness was cured, James' eyes were too bad for him to go back to being a secretary. William tried hard to find another job for James. He even thought of setting him up in business but finally just kept him on. His primary duty became playing the organ at family prayers!

William's softness toward his servants became a joke with his friends. When the Wilberforces were traveling one summer to the Lake District on vacation, William made sure his servants too were able to stay all night at the inns. Such consideration for the comfort of the hired help was almost unheard of.

Naturally, William's servants adored him. They ran the estate badly, but apparently William didn't care and Barbara didn't notice. Their friends noticed though! Once, after seeing an especially bad job by one of the servants, a friend asked William sharply, "Why don't you get rid of them? They aren't doing their jobs at all!"

"Oh, I couldn't fire them," William replied. "They are attached to us, and what would they do? They would have to go on charity!"

William's attitude toward keeping servants who needed work but were not doing a good job was typical of his attitude toward everyone. He was too kind to turn away anyone who came to ask for his help, whether he had invited them to come or not. There were always people coming to see William. He was too honest to let the servants tell these people he was out, because that would be encouraging the servants to lie. And it was a waste of time to tell people that William was busy. No one could believe William was so busy that he would not want to see them and hear about their problem. Most of the people who came wanted money or some sort of favor from him. William believed that since he had both money and a high position he owed it to God to help those not so fortunate.

William had closed the house in Wimbledon long ago and given the money to Hannah for her schools. He had also given money to Yorkshire charities and to friends who needed money. He always did this anonymously. "By careful management," William wrote, "I should be able to give at least one-quarter of my income to the poor."

Before his marriage, William had done even better than that in giving away his money. One year he actually gave away £3,000 more than his income had been!

After his marriage, William kept on giving away much of his money. Whenever he bought a property, he immediately lowered the rents to the tenant farmers by 30% to 40%.

Because of William's beliefs on the duty of the rich to help the poor, he always lived below the standard his friends expected of him. That never seemed to bother him a bit.

Barbara and William began their family quickly. In the first nine years of their marriage they had six children: William, Barbara, Elizabeth, Robert, Samuel and Henry.

Both Barbara and William believed that their first duty to their children was to see to their spiritual growth. Everyone, including the servants, spent ten minutes twice a day at prayers. James Burningham would begin to play the organ, the signal that prayers were about to start. The family came in, often one at a time, singing the hymn James was playing. Each person had a chair to kneel against, while William knelt against a table in the center. He was often shabbily dressed, according to one friend, and his clothes sometimes were put on crookedly because he never looked into a mirror. Since his eyes were too bad to let him see his image clearly, he didn't bother to look at all! William picked cheerful prayers to read. He felt they opened and closed the day properly for Christians.

Although William did not hold family prayer times to impress other people, his habits became known in the area and then in all of England. Many other families began to have prayer times too because of his and Barbara's example.

Despite Barbara's poor health and the strict religious atmosphere, the Wilberforce home was a happy one. There was always laughter and fun. People came and went, staying just for a meal or for a day, talking and enjoying being with the family. William did not want his children to grow up thinking that being a Christian meant you had to be stern and serious all the time.

William was an unusual father for his day. Most fathers who had the wealth and position he did rarely saw their children. Servants and a governess took care of the children, and they were to be out of sight most of the time. Instead, William insisted on eating as many meals as possible with the children, and he joined in their games. He played marbles and blindman's bluff and ran races with them. In the games the children treated him like one of them. One day, during a cricket game, a fast ball from young William hit his father on the foot. William was not able to walk for several days afterward, but it did not stop him from playing.

Barbara and William took their children traveling, to visit the British Museum, on picnics and to visit friends. And there were always other children in the neighborhood around them to play with too.

Later when the Wilberforce sons were in college, William stayed closely in touch with them and was interested in what they were doing. He wrote them many letters during those years, giving both news and advice.

Even while being a devoted father and husband, William was not neglecting his other interests. He had thought about writing a book for a long time and had even started it a few years before. He wanted to show that just saying you are a Christian, going to church on Sunday and living a decent life is not enough. William believed that Christianity must get into every corner of a person's life.

He had begun the book in 1793 before he had met Barbara. By 1797 he had finished the manuscript and had taken it to a publisher. The title was a long, boring one, but it told the reader just what the book was about. *A Practical View of the Prevailing Religious System of Professed Christians in the Higher and Middle Classes in This Country Contrasted with Real Christianity* was the name of William's book.

The publisher looked at the manuscript and shook his head. "A religious book written by a politician? It's unheard of! It will never sell!"

William should have been discouraged, but he quickly had a new idea to offer. "What if I sign every book?"

The publisher thought it over. People might buy a book that was personally signed by William Wilberforce. "All right. I'll print 500 copies."

The book came out two months later. It became an instant bestseller, and the 500 copies were quickly sold. In six months there were five printings, and a total of 7500 copies were sold. By 1826 the book had gone through fifteen printings in England and twenty-five in America, and had been translated into French, Italian, Spanish, Dutch and German.

William was glad his book was a good influence on so many people, but there was one man he had especially hoped it would change: William Pitt, his longtime friend. He sent Pitt an early copy and marked several places for his friend to read, but Pitt never became the kind of Christian William had hoped for.

7

First Victory Against Slavery

AS THE years passed William faithfully kept trying to get Parliament to pass a law forbidding the slave trade. In 1807 he tried again, as usual. This bill would make the carrying of slaves in British ships, anywhere in the Empire, illegal after May 1. Any British ship caught carrying slaves would be seized by the government.

The British Navy was the most powerful in the world. British ships ruled the oceans. William and his friends had no doubt that if the law were passed, the Navy would be able to enforce it.

On the night of February 23, the second reading of the Act for the Abolition of the Slave Trade was put before the House of Commons. It had already been passed in the House of Lords. The debate started calmly, but as it went on the Members became more enthusiastic. When one Member sat down after speaking for the bill, others would leap to their feet to continue the fight.

Sir Samuel Romilly, the Solicitor-General, gave the last speech. This man loved and admired William. He respected William not only for his stand on abolition but also for his work for penal reform and for better conditions for the poor.

In his speech Romilly became very emotional. He contrasted William Wilberforce with Napoleon Bonaparte. He brought the House to a peak of excitement when he made mention of the French leader, who was then seemingly at the height of human ambition and the pinnacle of earthly happiness. "Yet," Romilly told the House, "when Bonaparte goes to bed, his sleep must be tortured by the memory of the blood he has spilt and the oppressions he has committed to get where he is. William Wilberforce, on the other hand," Romilly went on, "will go home to his wife and happy family tonight, and he will know he has preserved many millions of his fellow creatures."

The elegance and animation of Romilly's speech, and his loving tribute to William, delighted the House. Suddenly a cry of "Hear! Hear!" rang out in the high-ceilinged hall. Other Members took up the shout as they rose to their feet in a standing ovation and turned to look at William.

Then, sounding above these cries and completely out of order in the staid old House, a new cheer began for William. "Hurrah! Hurrah! Hurrah!" Three "hurrahs" was one of the highest compliments an English crowd could pay any hero.

This was probably the greatest moment in William's fight against slavery, but he was sitting bent over in his seat, his head in his hands, with tears streaming down his face. The long-worked-for victory was at hand! And his colleagues in the House were loudly telling him how much respect and adoration they felt for him.

Later that night, still elated over the triumph, William jokingly asked Henry Thornton, "What should we abolish next?"

William spoke in jest, but Henry was serious when he said, "The Lottery, I think." He knew that the national lottery took money from those who could least afford it and gave back nothing but a unfounded dream of being rich.

Later William and the "Saints" did organize a campaign to persuade the government to give up the lottery. But it was not until 1826 that they were successful and the last state lottery was held.

Letters congratulating William and the Abolitionists on the passage of the bill poured in. As modest as ever, William felt that he was being given more honor than he deserved for his part in the victory. "I am only one among many fellow laborers," he said.

But the victory was far from a complete one. Slavery itself was not outlawed; only the trading and the carrying of slaves were illegal—and, of course, only in the British Empire. That meant that other nations could carry slaves on their ships as long as they did not go into British ports or the ports of British colonies. Thus, the United States was still a big and valuable market for slaves from Africa.

And now William faced another problem. A general election was called in late 1807, and it had him fighting for his seat in the House and his political life. Two men with plenty of money to spend wanted to oust him from his Yorkshire seat. One was a Whig, the other was a Tory, while William was an Independent.

In those days voters often had to travel a long way to vote, so the polls were actually open for two weeks—not just a day, the way they are now. It was the usual custom for candidates to "treat" voters to get their votes. "Treats" might be money, food, drink, or anything else a candidate thought would get the men to vote for him. "Treating" was one reason it cost so much to run for office, and those with the best "treats" often won the election.

William was against the idea of "treating," but when he saw what the others were doing, he reluctantly allowed his committee to go along. It was one of the few times in his life that William's actions might be questioned. But since his opponents and everyone else were doing the same thing, it was hardly noticed.

In the past William had not always acted like a politician, thinking ahead to how to get elected again. He had not visited Yorkshire often. He had not gone to the races or the other social affairs which he might have been expected to attend. And he did not ally himself with any of the rich or influential people there.

During this campaign, all the money William spent came from voluntary contributions. As an Independent he did not have the financial backing of a political party. The money came from people all around the country, however, not just those in Yorkshire. It was another evidence of the love and admiration people had for him.

It was a rough-and-tumble campaign. No holds were barred.

"Liar!" shouted hecklers during William's speeches.

William did not let that stop him from speaking out against slavery. "It is a national crime!" he told the voters. He went on to call it "one of the foulest blots ever to stain our national character."

During the days that the polls were open, Wil-

liam went from being hopeful of reelection to being
sure he had been beaten. But when the High Sher-
iff of Yorkshire, after a tense two hours of counting
the votes, declared William the winner, William
knew he had another chance to keep fighting slavery.

The next five years would be the prime of
William's work in Parliament and his influence on
the men who governed England. He went on with his
work to raise the standards of public life.

By 1811, however, William began to think that
representing Yorkshire in the House was getting to
be too much for him. He was thin and was taking
opium for pain. His doctor had prescribed the drug
twenty-one years earlier for pain and insomnia.
(Opium was a respected treatment in medical circles
at that time. Other drugs to relieve pain were not
yet known.)

At age 52, William's spirits were still high, and
he was as happy and cheerful as ever. But his body
was more frail.

If he resigned from his Yorkshire seat, he thought,
it would mean more time to spend with his family.
The children were growing up quickly, and while
he still spent as much time as possible with them,
he was also away a lot on House business.

One day William picked up one of his younger
sons. The boy suddenly began to cry. "He's always

afraid of strangers," the nurse told William. That probably helped William make his decision. In 1812 he resigned from Yorkshire, but he was quickly given the seat for Bramber, a much smaller and less important district. It would mean less correspondence for William and fewer visits from constituents who wanted something from him. However, William's opponents jumped on his resignation. "He didn't resign for his health or for his family!" they told everyone who would listen. "He resigned because he was afraid he would lose when another election is called!"

William's health was failing, despite all the doctors could do. He now had chest trouble in addition to the digestion problem he had fought for years. He was also developing a curvature of the spine. For this he had to wear a girdle-like steel frame. It was covered with leather for comfort, and had a part that supported his arms.

William did not tell anyone about the uncomfortable device. On one occasion, however, after visiting a friend, William accidently forgot to take his extra brace home with him, and the news got out. But pity for himself was not William's style. In his letter asking his friend to return the brace, he wrote, "How gracious God is in giving us such mitigations and helps for our infirmities." He could thank God in the midst of pain.

While the brace helped some, soon one of William's shoulders began to slope, and his head fell further forward each year until it was almost on his chest. It took much effort for him to raise his head. To a stranger, William might have looked somewhat grotesque, but he still had all his old charm, and he always seemed to have a smile on his face.

After 1812 William went down to the House of Commons less and less. Younger men were taking over now in the fights he had started. He still got there for the important meetings and debates when he was not sick, but now he had to be helped to his seat by the younger men. William's body was definitely getting weaker, but his mind was as sharp as ever. He followed every word of the main speeches. He not only cheered and groaned with the other Members, but he muttered comments on his own. Some were serious; others were humorous.

"He's our noisiest member," one of the younger men said. "He can make those sitting next to him shake with laughter!"

In another two years William's health had become so bad that Barbara would not let him travel. Even harder on William was the fact that his eyes, which had never been good, were now worse. He could not read the small print of the newspapers anymore, and he got tired of listening when others read to him.

In December of 1821 William and Barbara had another blow. Their oldest daughter, Barbara, died of tuberculosis. Even William's deep faith in God and heaven could not keep him from deep mourning. He felt he should somehow have been doing something to find a way to save her life.

In the House of Commons, other plans to abolish slavery came and went. A Slave Registration Bill passed that required planters to register their slaves. William thought that if the government kept a strict list of the number of slaves on each plantation, the owners would have to treat their slaves better. It did not work.

It was soon obvious that the planters would not improve the slaves' conditions on their own. Any improvement would have to come by law through Parliament. But even Parliament could not make laws for other countries!

As William got older, he began to see that the Abolitionists' approach to end the slave *trade,* instead of slavery *itself,* had been a mistake. He felt now that he and the others had been too cautious in their fight against slavery. He wished that they had tried to abolish all slavery throughout the Empire instead of just the trading of slaves and carrying them on British ships.

In 1825 the Anti-Slavery Society held an anniversary meeting. For the first time, William

Wilberforce was not among the speakers. He was ill at home. Young William was asked to say a few words for his father, but he broke down in tears. Another man had to leave the stage because he too was crying so hard, and a third was likewise overcome with emotion.

It was becoming obvious to everyone that William's leadership, accepted for more than forty years, was coming to an end. The problem was deciding who should take over the reins.

William chose the man: Thomas Buxton, a little-known and not very experienced Member of the House of Commons. Some people wondered at the choice, but again William showed that he knew what he was doing.

Buxton's religious background was similar to William's, but Buxton had not been born rich. He had worked in a brewery for several years before being elected to Parliament in 1818. The two men did not look alike, either. Buxton was a big man and was an athlete who loved sports. He had once swum out to a ship wrecked in a gale to rescue a drowning sailor, proving his courage in a crisis.

Now that William had chosen the man to lead the battle for "Emancipation of the Slaves," he could relax and take things a little easier.

8

Time to Retire

IN THE spring of 1824 William got sick again. This time it was a serious lung infection, probably pneumonia.

"He may not recover this time," the doctors warned his worried family. "Bed rest is necessary." For three weeks William stayed in bed. Sometimes his cough was so bad that he was not allowed to speak unless it was absolutely necessary. And speak was what William wanted to do—and not just to his family. He wanted to speak to Parliament and to the country.

The last entry he had written in his diary before he got sick tells why speaking now was so important to him. The entry read, "Poor Smith, the missionary, died in prison in Demerara! The day of reckoning will come!" William wanted desperately to be part of that "day of reckoning."

John Smith had been a missionary to Demerara, in British Guiana, the former Dutch colony in South America, now owned by England. He was the only minister for 78,000 slaves, and had only a small chapel on one of the plantations for a church. Smith hated slavery and tried to bring Christianity and better living conditions to the blacks. But everything he planned in order to help the slaves have a better life was blocked by the white planters.

Smith also had tuberculosis, and the climate in that part of the world made it worse. He was about to give up and go back to England when the slaves rebelled against their owners.

Somehow, the slaves had found out that a message about them had been sent from England to the Governor. A rumor began and spread quickly among the slaves about it.

"Maybe it says we are free," many whispered.

"That can't be," others argued.

"But if it's not freedom, why don't the white men tell us what was in it?"

The dispatch from London had not given the slaves their freedom as they hoped. It was a new regulation that limited the whipping of slaves. The white owners, who saw the whip and the threat of it as the sign of their authority, and thought it was vital to keeping order, did not want to tell the slaves about the new, more humane law.

The actual revolt began on August 18, 1823, on two plantations. Once started, it spread quickly to other plantations. The Governor came to try to talk to the slaves, but they would not accept anything but complete and unconditional freedom. The Governor gave up on diplomacy and turned to force to end the uprising.

The blacks were poorly armed and had no real leadership. It took only three days to brutally put down their rebellion. During the fighting only one white man was killed, for while the blacks were temporarily in control of their plantations, they were not cruel or revengeful. They locked up their white masters, putting some of them into the stocks, but they did not torture or kill them. Nor did they loot or burn the houses or barns as the whites had been afraid they would.

Unfortunately, the whites did not follow the same humane principles. When the revolt was crushed, almost fifty slaves were hanged. Others were given the feared punishment of one thousand lashes or were condemned to work in chains. One slave was sentenced to work in chains for the rest of his life. The planters meant to send a message to any other slaves who were thinking of trying to get free.

Once the danger to the planters was over, they arrested the missionary, John Smith. He was accused of knowing in advance what the slaves were planning but not warning the whites. Whether or not Smith knew ahead of time what the slaves were planning is still a mystery. It was never proved at his trial, however.

If the missionary had been told in advance by the blacks of the planned revolt, it would have put him in a no-win situation. If he went to the authorities and told them what was coming, many of the people he had been preaching to about Christ would be arrested and tortured. On the other hand, if he knew about the revolt and did not go to the white officials with a warning, many more deaths, both black and white, could come in the fighting.

Smith was given a court martial instead of a jury trial. The excuse for this kind of trial was that he would not be able to get a fair hearing from a jury of the white planters. No blacks, of course, could serve on juries.

The laws that Smith was tried under were a strange mixture of the old Dutch laws, which had never been taken off the books, and the newer English laws. The whites did not care which law was used as long as it favored them.

Slaves condemned to punishment were allowed to testify against Smith although slaves were not usually allowed to testify in court. This and other questionable methods were used against Smith. So he was declared guilty and sentenced to death.

Smith's wife was not allowed to visit him in prison as he awaited execution. In the meantime, the Governor decided to refer the whole case back to England. Before they could get an answer from Britain, however, Smith died in prison from natural causes. Ironically, the British government had meant to give him a reprieve.

The whole incident of John Smith and his case was to be discussed in the House of Commons, and William was eager to play his part.

"I very much wish," he said, "if my voice should be strong enough, to bear my testimony against the scandalous injustice against poor Smith."

On June 1 William, still weak from his long illness and bed rest, pulled himself out of bed and went to the House of Commons to speak. The galleries were packed with spectators, but the floor of the House, where the Members sat, was almost empty.

"They've all gone to the roofs of St. James," William was told. "A man and his wife are about to ascend in a balloon and they are watching."

The debate was postponed for ten days. When the debate did start, other Abolitionists carried the burden of the speeches. William made only a short talk, and he was not happy with it. "I quite forgot my topics for a speech and made sad work of it," he wrote in disgust.

The Abolitionists did win the sympathy of the country with their story of John Smith, however, and they considered this an important victory.

Years after these debates in the House of Commons, an official of the London Missionary Society found an old bill sent by Smith for money for his trial. In very tiny letters he had written "2 Corinthians 4:8–9" on the bill. Turning to the Bible, the official read, "We are troubled on every side, yet not distressed; we are perplexed, but not in despair, persecuted but not forsaken; cast down, but not destroyed." It had been the missionary's last message and witness of his faith.

William's speech on John Smith was his last major speech in the House. A few days later he introduced another petition in favor of Emancipation, but these were his last speeches to his fellow Members.

William's disappointment with his speech on John Smith, along with his poor health, made him stop to wonder if it was time for him to step down and resign his seat in the House of Commons. He had served there many years, and there were younger men in the House now to take over.

Some of these younger Members were the sons of the men who had stood beside William in the fight against slavery. They had the energy William had once had, and they were ready to take over the leadership positions.

Now the "Saints" were looked up to by many Members who were not religious, but who believed that the way the "Saints" voted on a bill would be the "right" way.

William was not sure he could do anything more if he stayed in the House, although he knew he could probably keep his seat as long as he wanted.

"Why not just cut down on the days you spend in the House?" friends asked. "That way you could conserve your strength."

"Just come for the most important debates," others argued.

But William could not give less than one hundred percent to his work. He was too conscientious to work at his job only "part-time."

While he was still considering the pros and cons of resigning, William got sick again. This time he was in bed for a month, and his health was so bad that he had to take it easy for the rest of the year.

"You've had two serious illnesses in the last year," his family reminded him. "Give up public life before it kills you!"

William had to admit his family was right. His doctor would not *order* him not to go back to the House, but he hinted strongly that if William got sick again, it might be his last illness.

William also felt he could do as much now for

the cause of Emancipation from home as he could in the House. He would write articles and pamphlets and still speak at various rallies.

There might be an alternative solution, though. William's friend, Sir John Sinclair, suggested it.

"You can accept a peerage. Then you'll be in the House of Lords. That way you'd still be in government, but the atmosphere in that House is much calmer than what you have seen in the Commons."

For most men, the idea of being made a "Peer of the Realm" would be welcome, especially since it would mean being able to stay in one of the two Houses of government. There was no question that William could have had the honor if he had agreed to it. But he refused.

"As I have done nothing to make it naturally come to me, I would have to endeavor to go to it, and this would be carving out for myself much more than a Christian ought to do," he explained.

There was another reason William was not interested in becoming a Member of the House of Lords. If he were there, his children would be thrown into that level of society, and William was afraid their religion might suffer in that environment. As a father, he was still concerned about his children's beliefs and actions.

When William finally made his decision to retire from the House of Commons, one of the happiest people was his wife, Barbara. She had worried for so many years about his health, and felt so strongly that his work in Parliament was to blame for much of his illness, that she saw his retirement as a victory.

In February 1825 William retired from the House of Commons where he had served for 45 years. He had much to look back on. Despite his frail body and many serious illnesses, he had out-lived most of his friends from the early days, in-cluding his old friend, William Pitt, who had died in 1806.

All of England recognized him as the leader of the "Saints," and even his political enemies respected him.

He was known around the world as a freedom fighter for the slaves. He had been introduced to the Emperor of Russia and the King of Prussia in London. He had written long letters to Talleyrand, the French statesman, and been made an honorary citizen of France.

William Wilberforce and his work were known everywhere, especially in America. William had writ-ten to President Jefferson in 1807 suggesting to the slave-owning American that the two countries work together for the abolition of slavery. He had also been friends with John Jay and Charles Pinckney, both American ambassadors to England.

William had not been able to free the slaves, but he had seen some strides toward the goal. He believed the time of total Emancipation of the slaves was near. And he had not neglected his other aim in life: to raise the morals of the country.

Just before William left the House of Commons for the last time, one of the other "Saints" said to him, "It must be a satisfaction to have observed that the moral tone of the House of Commons, as well as of the nation, is much higher than when you first entered public life; and there can be no doubt God has made you the honored instrument of contributing much to this great improvement."

William had often been accused by his enemies of being falsely modest, but they were wrong. His modesty and humility were real, not pretended or put on for effect. His journal has many comments about his weaknesses as he fought to keep himself from falling into believing the praise, admiration and honors he received.

Everything William did came from his deep Christian faith. He thought of himself first as a spiritual leader, then as a legislator. He knew he had not done as much as he could have in his time of leadership. It is not likely, however, that anyone could have done more.

9

———◆———

Hard Times

AFTER leaving the House of Commons, William and Barbara went house hunting again. This time they chose Highwood Hill, an estate near the little village of Mill Hill.

"It will be a retreat beyond the bounds of the metropolis," William said.

Highwood Hill was an estate of about 140 acres with a comfortably large brick house, several cottages and the farm. A big advantage for William was that it was only a short distance from the main road, making it easy for visitors to get to. He had given up his seat in the Commons, but he was not going to give up visits from friends.

As he had always done, William immediately lowered the rents of the tenant farmers. Then he discovered that the new chapel he thought was to be built nearby was not going to be built after all. This was a blow to William, since the nearest church was more than three miles away, a long distance to go for services.

"We'll build a chapel for us and for the village," William decided.

At first the local vicar was enthusiastic. Then he changed his mind. He did not want a new chapel to be built. He verbally attacked William, calling him a liar, hypocrite and a man inspired only by money.

William took these attacks as calmly and patiently as he had taken so many political attacks before. He kept on with his plans for the chapel.

A few friends sent William money for the project, but his own funds paid most of the cost of the church. It was to be for the villagers, the tenants and the Wilberforces to worship in. Because of the vicar's opposition, the building of the chapel went slowly. It actually did not open until a few days after William's death, although it was finished while he was still living.

Highwood Hill was a comfortable home, and William was sure he would live there the rest of his life. But it did not turn out that way.

The oldest Wilberforce son, William Jr., had studied to be a lawyer, but he had been told by his doctor—backed by his father and a close friend—that he would not make a good lawyer. Young William was a heavy man and had a "delicate stomach." "He should have outdoor work," the doctor said.

Young William had fallen in love with the daughter of the Bible Society's secretary and married her. The woman's family had no money, and young William had no job. They moved in with Barbara and William.

"I can manage the farm," young William told his father. It sounded like the perfect solution. The farm was not making money and needed management. William needed to work outside for his health. If he managed the farm, it would solve both problems.

Soon he began looking for something that would help make up for the losses the farm was having.

"I've met a Major Close," young William told his father. "He believes a dairy farm and retail business at St. John's Wood would make a good partnership for him and for us. It's on the edge of London, only three miles south of here; he would run the project and I'd furnish the money. I'd only have to ride over every week or so to check on it."

Major Close apparently convinced William as well as his son, and the two Wilberforces decided to invest in the plan. William allowed his son to put in the money from his inheritance. Then he himself borrowed £6,000 from a cousin to get the dairy business off the ground. With this investment, plus the cost of building the new chapel, William's finances were dangerously low.

But the worst was yet to come. The dairy did not work out, and young William secretly borrowed more money to keep it going. By 1829 the losses were so large it didn't seem possible to ever earn them back. But young William did not want to admit he had failed in this as well as in being a lawyer. He refused to quit, and for the next 18 months things got worse and worse.

When the Wilberforces gave up on the dairy business, they had a debt of £50,000. Since most of this was young William's debt, he and his family left England and went to Europe to get away from his creditors.

William Wilberforce was now old and his health was bad. But he took on his son's debt.

"I have to," he told himself and Barbara. "If I don't agree to pay what William owes, he will never be able to come back to England. He will be an exile the rest of his life! I can't let that happen to my son. He's my oldest and has my name."

When William's old friends heard about the situation, six of them offered to pay off the debt for him. Even an enemy from the old days in the House of Commons, Lord Fitzwilliam, wanted to help. But William would not accept their offer.

To raise money to pay off the debt, William had to sell Highwood Hill. He loved the estate but could no longer afford it.

Even harder for William was the fact that he finally had to let all his servants go except for one man, a maid and a reader he had to have now to read the newspapers and other papers to him.

As always William worried about these old and faithful, if not efficient, servants. They were not fit to get new jobs, so he sold the lands he still owned in York. That gave him enough money to take care of his servants in their old age.

"Where will we go?" Barbara asked. There was no money to buy another house.

The other three Wilberforce sons were now all ministers with churches of their own. William and Barbara were dependent on their sons' generosity and spent the rest of their lives moving from one son's home to another. They also spent time visiting other relatives and friends for short periods, as they had done in the past.

Young William never accepted the blame for the failure of the farm and dairy. William refused, however, to let their relationship be anything but a good one.

One of the hardest things for William, now that he had no home, was that he had no place to invite his friends to come for a meal or for overnight. But he took his hard times in his usual philosophical way and with complete faith in God.

"I can scarce understand why my life has been spared so long, unless it be to show that a man can be as happy without a fortune as with one," he said.

Barbara was not as cheerful or accepting. She did not like having to live with her sons and especially with their wives. Robert had a special cottage built for his parents so that his wife and Barbara would not have to live in the same house. Robert also had a special garden made for his father.

William loved to wander along the walk in this garden. His small body was more and more stooped, but his spirits were as lively as ever. He could not recognize the flowers now because of his bad eyesight, but he could still talk.

In 1830 he spoke to a crowd of 2,000 at an antislavery rally. He was frail and bent, and his voice was weaker, but he was the one man the people wanted to hear.

William felt sure this would be his last public speech, and when his daughter, Lizzie, died in childbirth in 1832, he was sure of it.

But after another general election, William was talked into proposing another petition against slavery.

"I never thought to appear in public again," he began his speech, "but it shall never be said that William Wilberforce is silent while the slaves require his help." It was April 1833.

William looked smaller and more twisted than

ever now, but some of his old enthusiasm and spirit came back as he spoke.

He was almost through his speech. "I trust we now approach the very end of our career," he was saying when a sudden shaft of sunlight came through the window, dramatically lighting his face. William's old gift of words and timing came back. He looked at the beam, then at the audience. "This light from heaven," he shouted with all his old fire, "is the earnest of our success!"

After that speech, William's health kept getting worse. In the early summer of 1833 he got influenza. He could not seem to get rid of its effects, and he finally decided to go to Bath to take the waters there again. They had always helped him before—maybe they would be the answer again.

William's son Henry went with him. Henry kept his brothers up to date on their father's condition, but it was not good news. In early July William's knees and thighs were so swollen, Henry wrote, that he could not wear his regular trousers. He had had to have a special pair made that were extra large and extra loose.

William accepted all these problems with his usual fortitude. He looked for things to be thankful for: he was not in great pain; he could sleep; his servants took care of him; his friends came to visit; and most important, he was still with his family.

From Bath, William moved to a cousin's house in London to be nearer his doctor. For a short time the doctor thought William might be getting better and needed only a short rest.

Every morning William was wheeled outside to breathe in the fresh air for about ten minutes before morning prayers and breakfast. After that, he lay on a sofa in a back room to receive friends. Barbara fussed and complained about all the people who visited, and she stood guard. Sometimes she refused to let some people go in, and she ordered others to leave when she saw that William was getting tired.

The house which William was staying in was only about a mile from Westminster where the Slavery Abolition Bill was being debated. Each day messengers came to give William the news of its progress.

While William's friends were shocked at his appearance now, he was still alert, cheerful and eagerly waiting for news of the debate in Parliament. It was agreed by everyone that if the Bill got past the House of Commons, it would be approved quickly by the House of Lords.

On Thursday, July 25, 1833, William finally got the news he had been waiting for most of his adult life: Abolition had finally been carried!

The bill was not a complete victory, though. It dealt only with the West Indies and not the whole

British Empire. Also, the only slaves who would be free right away were those under six years old. The others would have to wait a year, until midnight, July 31, 1834, for their complete freedom. After that, the blacks would have to work three-fourths of the day for their old masters for food and clothing for seven more years. (Later that was reduced to just five years.) The government also agreed to pay compensation to the slave owners for the loss of their labor. But all the slaves were on their way to freedom at last. William's lifework was finished.

Saturday William became weaker. His mind was calm, but his body was failing. Sunday he was worse. Late that night Henry and Barbara heard him whisper, "I am in a very distressed state."

"Yes," Henry said reassuringly, "but you have your feet on the Rock."

Even in his last hours William was humble. "I do not venture to speak so positively," he murmured, "but I hope I have." A few hours later, at 3 a.m., Monday, July 29, 1833, William Wilberforce died.

As soon as the news of his death got out, the Members of the House of Commons asked the family to let them bury William in Westminster Abbey.

On August 3, the body was carried into the Abbey by two Royal Dukes, the Lord Chancellor, the

Speaker of the House of Commons and four Peers. Members of both Houses of Parliament walked in the procession, and thousands of people in the city wore mourning.

William was laid to rest in the north wall near the tombs of William Pitt the younger and Charles Fox. It was an unheard-of honor for a private citizen who had been retired so long from Parliament.

The funeral itself was a simple service. The only exception was the presence of the glorious Choir of the Abbey. That was the way William would have wanted it.

Not only England honored William Wilberforce when he died, but America did also. Here slavery would last another thirty years. But members of the Phoenix Society, a Negro self-improvement group in the North, wore badges of mourning for a month after William's death. A New York group sent a letter of sympathy to the family. In Newark, New Jersey, one of the self-improvement groups held a memorial service, and at the Baptist meetinghouse in Boston a commemorative address was given. In Philadelphia too Negroes assembled in solemn tribute to William.

The obituary in the York *Herald* summed up William's life when it said, on August 3, 1833, "His warfare is accomplished, his course is finished, he kept the faith."

10

The Work and Name Live On

WILLIAM Wilberforce was dead. His voice would not be heard again in the House of Commons. But like many people who have done great things in their lives, his death did not mean the end of his work. And it certainly did not mean the forgetting of his name. His work and name live on—even today, more than a century and a half after his burial in Westminster Abbey.

During his lifetime, William and his fellow "Saints" changed the House of Commons and its image forever. Before William came, the common people did not have much respect for politicians. They never thought of them as having any Christian virtues, and they considered government a corrupt business. The Members saw themselves as above the common people and saw the House of Commons as a sort of exclusive country club. They saw nothing wrong in doing whatever it took to keep their seats there. They were concerned with passing laws that helped the rich, not with the serious work of helping make the country better.

The "Saints" changed that. By their example and efforts, they turned the House around. It became a group of real leaders who were more concerned with the good of the nation than with themselves.

In 1837 Victoria became Queen of England. During the 64 years she was on the throne, William became one of the country's biggest heroes. His life and work were included in schoolbooks. Many young men, after reading about his life and faith, decided to go into politics and be like him in their service to others.

Assisted by the other Evangelicals, William had also made the country see that they were wrong in the way they treated not only black slaves but also the peoples of Africa and India that Britain now ruled. England, William had shown, had an obligation to help all these native peoples.

Thanks to William and his friends, countries around the world had been made to think about the evils of slavery. Some nations, including Mexico, Colombia and Brazil, had begun efforts to free the slaves even before William's death. Others did not act as quickly but later followed the emancipation examples.

Slaves in the French colonies were set free in 1848. The Portuguese began, in 1858, a twenty-year program of training for the slaves, who would then be freed.

In America, it took a long and bloody Civil War between the states to free the slaves in the South, but that too was finally accomplished.

William's name became widely known not only in England and Europe, but also in Canada and the United States. Here is one exmple of this:

About 1830 the city of Cincinnati, Ohio, decided to start enforcing some old laws about blacks that were on its books. One of these demanded a $500 bond from every black coming into the city. Since Cincinnati was on the northern, or "free," side of the Ohio River, it was a goal for many runaway slaves. The bond had not been required for many years, but with more and more blacks coming into the city, the white citizens began to be afraid. They wanted the laws to be enforced, or the blacks to leave.

Few of the blacks had the $500 to give. "We'll go to Canada," some of them declared. Canada had no restrictions, and the Ohio blacks were able to get land in Ontario near the town of London. But many of the ex-slaves did not want to leave their homes to go so far away again.

Then a white mob took the law into their own

hands. They moved into the black section of the city, and for three days there was fear and rioting. It was the final straw for many of the blacks. They changed their minds and headed north.

The colony these free blacks started was named after the freedom fighter from England: Wilberforce.

The settlement was never very large, but it became a symbol to the world of what blacks could do if they were given the chance. They organized a local government, and set up churches, schools and businesses. Some farmed the land they had been allotted. Each one could keep what he earned.

But the colony's leaders started to fight among themselves, and the settlement began to fail. By 1878 only four of the original founders or their families were left, and the name of the town had been changed.

Today there is still a town of Wilberforce on the map of Ontario. It is not connected with the original colony and is to the northeast, near the town of Bancroft.

In the United States, William's name is still honored at a university in the town of Wilberforce, Ohio. The school was founded before the Civil War by blacks who knew of Wilberforce's work in England, and of the Wilberforce Colony in Canada. Although Wilberforce University was originally started to educate blacks, it has always been open to all races.

But it is in England that William Wilberforce is best remembered. Many of the places he lived during his life have disappeared, of course. But the house in Hull where he was born has survived and is now the Wilberforce House Museum. Many mementos of his life and work are on display there. Every year visitors and tourists come from around the world to learn more about William's life.

Less noticeable tributes exist in areas where William once lived. The road leading to the houses that have been built where his home in Wimbledon stood is called "Wilberforce Way." The site of the oak tree where William Pitt challenged his friend to start his work of freeing the slaves is marked with a plaque.

Perhaps the best known and most visible tribute to William is in the north aisle of Westminster Abbey. Here is a statue of William Wilberforce, done by Samuel Joseph in 1840. William is seated, his legs crossed and his head bent forward, but looking up as he gazes out over the Abbey.

Whether or not William would have liked the statue no one knows. But it is certain that he would have heartily approved the epitaph on it. After listing all the works William did in his lifetime, the epitaph ends:

". . . til, through the merits of *JESUS CHRIST*, his only redeemer and Savior (whom in his life and in his writings he had desired to glorify), he shall rise in the resurrection of the just."

This book was produced by CLC Publications. We hope it has been life-changing and has given you a fresh experience of God through the work of the Holy Spirit. CLC Publications is an outreach of CLC Ministries International, a global literature mission with work in over 50 countries. If you would like to know more about us or are interested in opportunities to serve with a faith mission, we invite you to contact us at:

CLC Ministries International
PO Box 1449
Fort Washington, PA 19034

Phone: (215) 542-1242
E-mail: clcmail@clcusa.org
Website: www.clcusa.org

DO YOU LOVE GOOD CHRISTIAN BOOKS?
Do you have a heart for worldwide missions?

You can receive a FREE subscription to
CLC's newsletter on global literature missions
Order by e-mail at:

clcheartbeat@clcusa.org
or fill in the coupon below and mail to:

P.O. Box 1449
Fort Washington, PA 19034

FREE *HEARTBEAT* SUBSCRIPTION!

Name: _____

Address:_____

_____

Phone: _____ Email:_____

READ THE REMARKABLE STORY OF
the founding of
CLC International

"Any who doubt that Elijah's God still lives ought to read of the money supplied when needed, the stores and houses provided, and the appearance of personnel in answer to prayer."

—Moody Monthly

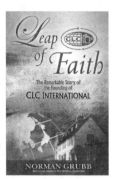

Is it possible that the printing press, the editor's desk, the Christian bookstore, and the mail order department, can glow with the fast-moving drama of an "Acts of the Apostles"?

Find out, as you are carried from two people in an upstairs bookroom to a worldwide chain of Christian bookcenters and publishing, multiplied by only a "shoestring" of faith and committed, though unlikely, lives.

Read all the titles in the
FAITH'S ADVENTURERS SERIES

from CLC Publications

True stories of Christians throughout history who dared
to live by faith, and their adventures in following God:

- *Thomas J. Barnardo*
- *William Carey*
- *Fanny Crosby*
- *Mabel Francis*
- *Ann H. Judson*
- *Ira Sankey*
- *Hudson Taylor*
- *John Bunyan*
- *Nancy Chapel*
- *Ed and Doreen Dulka*
- *Grace Livingstone Hill*
- *Helen Roseveare*
- *Billy Sunday*
- *William Wilberforce*

Collect all 14 titles!

Ann H. Judson
of Burma
ISBN 0-87508-601-2

Colombian Jungle Escape
(Ed and Doreen Dulka)
ISBN 0-87508-092-8

Father to Nobody's Children
(*Thomas J. Barnardo*)
ISBN 0-87508-662-4

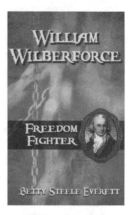

William Wilberforce –
Freedom Fighter
ISBN 978-0-87508-976-8

Gracious Writer
for God
(*Grace Livingstone Hill*)
ISBN 0-87508-664-0

Ira Sankey:
First Gospel singer
(*Ira Sankey*)
ISBN 0-87508-471-0

God's Tinker
(*John Bunyan*)
ISBN 0-87508-462-1

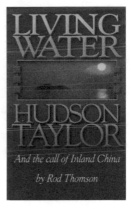

Living Water
(*Hudson Taylor*)
ISBN 0-87508-666-7

Only One Life
(*Mabel Francis*)
ISBN 0-87508-667-5

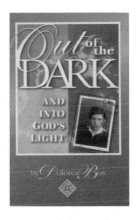

Out of the Dark
(*Nancy Chapel*)
ISBN 0-87508-720-5

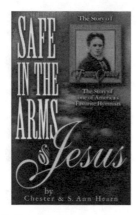

Safe in the Arms of Jesus
(*Fanny Crosby*)
ISBN 0-87508-665-9

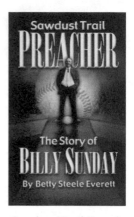

Sawdust Trail Preacher
(*Billy Sunday*)
ISBN 0-87508-499-0

Though Lions Roar
(*Helen Roseveare*)
ISBN 0-87508-663-2

William Carey:
Missionary Pioneer
ISBN 0-87508-187-8